W9-AET-978

HISTORY'S GREATEST RIVALS

ULYSSES S. GRANT **Vs.** ROBERT E. LEE

CIVIL WAR RIVALS

Ellis Roxburgh

Gareth Stevens
PUBLISHING

Please visit our website, **www.garethstevens.com**. For a free color catalog of all our high-quality books, call toll-free 1-800-542-2595 or fax 1-877-542-2596.

Library of Congress Cataloging-in-Publication Data

Roxburgh, Ellis.
 Ulysses S. Grant vs. Robert E. Lee : Civil War rivals / Ellis Roxburgh.
    pages cm. — (History's greatest rivals)
 Includes index.
 ISBN 978-1-4824-2227-6 (pbk.)
 ISBN 978-1-4824-2228-3 (6 pack)
 ISBN 978-1-4824-2225-2 (library binding)
 1. United States—History—Civil War, 1861-1865—Juvenile literature. I. Title.
 E468.R795 2015
 973.7—dc23

                          2014035917

Published in 2015 by
Gareth Stevens Publishing
111 East 14th Street, Suite 349
New York, NY 10003

© 2015 Brown Bear Books Ltd

For Brown Bear Books Ltd:
Editorial Director: Lindsey Lowe
Managing Editor: Tim Cooke
Children's Publisher: Anne O'Daly
Design Manager: Keith Davis
Designer: Mary Walsh and Karen Perry
Picture Manager: Sophie Mortimer

Picture Credits
Front Cover: Shutterstock: background; TopFoto: Ullsteinbild left, Granger Collection right.

Library of Congress: 6, 7, 8, 9, 14, 18, 19, 20, 21, 23, 24, 25, 26, 28, 29, 30, 32, 33, 34, 35, 36, 40, 41, 45; Robert Hunt Library: 4/5, 42/43; TopFoto: Granger Collection 5, 44; Ullsteinbild 4, 42; U.S. Army Center of Military History: 22; U.S. National Archives: ifc, 10, 11, 13, 15, 16, 27, 31, 37, 38, 39. Artistic Effects Shutterstock

Brown Bear Books has made every attempt to contact the copyright holder. If anyone has any information please contact licensing@brownbearbooks.co.uk

All artwork: © Brown Bear Books

Manufactured in the United States of America
CPSIA compliance information: Batch #CW15GS. For further information contact Gareth Stevens, New York, New York at 1-800-542-2595.

CONTENTS

AT ODDS

Ulysses S. Grant (1822-1885) was an unlikely man to lead the Union to victory. When the Civil War began, he was thought unfit for service—but he soon challenged that idea.

✳ Grant rose to take command of US forces in Tennessee.

✳ Victories at Fort Donelson and the Battle of Shiloh in 1862 brought Grant to the notice of President Abraham Lincoln.

✳ Lincoln promoted Grant, saying, "I cannot spare this man. He fights!"

✳ Grant led a successful final campaign to grind down the South.

✳ Grant later served two terms as US president.

Robert E. Lee (1807-1870) commanded the Confederate Army of Northern Virginia. Although he was ultimately defeated, he proved that he was one of the most brilliant military commanders in history.

* Lee had been superintendent of West Point military academy. He taught many of those who fought for and against him in the Civil War.

* Lee opposed secession, but was loyal to his home state so fought for the South.

* Lee won a series of remarkable victories, despite the Union having more men and better equipment.

* Lee invaded the North twice to try to achieve a decisive victory.

* Lee only surrendered when his Army of Northern Virginia nearly ran out of supplies.

CONTEXT

By 1853, the United States had spread across the whole North American continent. But the rapid expansion of the country had highlighted the deep and irreconcilable divisions among Americans over the institution of slavery.

In the industrial states of the North, slavery had been outlawed. In the South, however, slavery was the basis of an agricultural economy that relied on huge plantations growing tobacco, sugar, and cotton.

WHIPPING: A white man whips a slave in the background as others work.

$200 Reward.

RANAWAY from the subscriber, on the night of Thursday, the 30th of Sepember.

FIVE NEGRO SLAVES,

To-wit : one Negro man, his wife, and three children.

The man is a black negro, full height, very erect, his face a little thin.   He is about forty years of age, and calls himself *Washington Reed*, and is known by the name of Washington.   He is probably well dressed, possibly takes with him an ivory headed cane, and is of good address.   Several of his teeth are gone.

Mary, his wife, is about thirty years of age, a bright mulatto woman, and quite stout and strong.

The oldest of the children is a boy, of the name of FIELDING, twelve years of age, a dark mulatto, with heavy eyelids. He probably wore a new cloth cap.

MATILDA, the second child, is a girl, six years of age, rather a dark mulatto, but a bright and smart looking child.

MALCOLM, the youngest, is a boy, four years old, a lighter mulatto, ... bright. He probably also wore a cloth cap. If examined, ... will be found to be ... Washington and Mary have lived at or near St. Louis, ... It is supposed that they are making their way to Chicago ...

POSTER: This notice offers a reward
for the return of runaway slaves.

The US government introduced the Missouri Compromise of 1820 (renewed in 1850). This ensured that every new slave state admitted to the Union would be balanced by a new free state, to maintain equal representation in the government. But the Kansas–Nebraska Act of 1854 allowed new states to choose whether to be free or slave states. Kansas became a battleground between pro- and antislavers.

Growing Tension

In 1857, the US Supreme Court ruled in the case *Scott vs. Stanford* that Dred Scott,

> " You had better, all you people of the South, prepare yourselves for a settlement of this question, that must come up for settlement sooner than you are prepared for it. "
>
> John Brown, 1859

a slave whose owners had taken him to a free state, did not have to be freed. The ruling reinforced the legal status of slavery and declared that black slaves were not US citizens.

John Brown's Raid

On October 16, 1859, the abolitionist John Brown raided the arsenal at Harper's Ferry, West Virginia. He wanted to seize weapons to arm a slave revolt. Soldiers commanded by Colonel Robert E. Lee arrested him. Brown's trial and execution inflamed the slavery debate still further. In 1860, the presidential candidate for the new Republican Party, Abraham Lincoln, ran on an anti-slavery platform. His party was popular in the North but Southerners were terrified that, if Lincoln won the election, he would abolish slavery.

> " Those who deny freedom to others, deserve it not for themselves; and, under a just God, cannot long retain it. "

Abraham Lincoln, April 6, 1859

ELECTION: Abraham Lincoln (left) appears on this poster from the 1864 presidential election, when he ran for president again.

CELEBRATION: South Carolinians in Charleston celebrate secession from the Union.

Lincoln Becomes President

Lincoln won the 1860 presidential election, thanks to votes from the North. However, before the new president had even moved into the White House, seven Southern states had left, or seceded from, the Union, led by South Carolina. Another four states soon followed. The seceding states formed a new nation, the Confederate States of America. They elected a president, Jefferson Davis, and made Richmond, Virginia, their capital city.

The Confederate leaders demanded that all Union soldiers be removed from former federal sites in the Confederacy. Lincoln refused to withdraw the troops. He did not recognize the South's right to leave the Union. The two sides were on a collision course.

ULYSSES S. GRANT

Born into relative poverty, Grant was only an average student at West Point, and had a mediocre early military career.

Ulysses S. Grant's early life showed no hint of his outstanding later career. He was only an average student at the US Military Academy at West Point, then he served in the Mexican War (1846–1848). His early military career was marred by an alcohol problem, and he resigned from the army in 1854.

An Exceptional Soldier

Grant volunteered when war began in 1861 but was turned down. Later, he was accepted and given command of a regiment of volunteers. His first success was the capture of Fort Donelson, Tennessee, in February 1862, followed by the Battle of Shiloh. Lincoln admired Grant's aggressive fighting. He was nicknamed "Unconditional Surrender" Grant.

Total Defeat

As other Union generals failed to take the fight to the South, Lincoln promoted Grant. In October 1863, he became commander in the West. After Grant's victories at Vicksburg

FAITH: Grant inspired great loyalty from President Abraham Lincoln.

SCRUFFY: Grant was well known for his lack of formality and care in his own appearance.

and Chattanooga, Lincoln made him general-in-chief of all Union armies in March 1864. Grant finally forced Robert E. Lee to surrender on April 2, 1865.

The Nation's Hero

Grant was promoted to full general in 1866 in recognition of his contribution to the Union victory. In 1868, he was elected to serve as the 18th President of the United States. He held office for two terms (1869–1877) but a series of scandals damaged his presidency. His reputation was eventually restored with the publication of his Civil War memoirs, completed just a month before his death on July 23, 1885.

> " No terms except an unconditional and immediate surrender can be accepted. "
>
> **Ulysses S. Grant, 1862**

ROBERT E. LEE

Unlike Grant, Robert E. Lee was from a leading family. An outstanding student, he was famous for his smart appearance.

Lee was born into a wealthy Virginia family. His father was a general who served with George Washington in the American Revolution (1775–1783). Lee attended the US Military Academy at West Point and graduated second in his year in 1829. He remains the only West Point graduate never to receive a single demerit for misconduct.

TRAVELLER: Lee watches his troops from his beloved horse, Traveller.

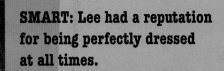

SMART: Lee had a reputation for being perfectly dressed at all times.

A Hard Choice

When civil war became inevitable, Lincoln offered Lee command of the US armies. Lee decided he could not fight his home state, and joined the Confederacy. He resigned from the US Army and was put in charge of Virginia's army and navy. In June 1862, he took command of the Army of Northern Virginia.

An Outstanding Commander

Lee was an imaginative strategic leader and his army enjoyed a string of victories. After his defeat at Gettysburg in July 1863, however, Lee was on the defensive until his surrender in April 1865. After the war, Lee worked to help reunite the country. He died in October 1870.

> " I can anticipate no greater calamity for the country than a dissolution of the Union. "
>
> Robert E. Lee, 1861

UPHOLDING THE UNION

» POLITICIANS AND SUBORDINATES

Grant relied on his own judgment to decide battle strategy, but he also knew he needed the support of Union politicians and his own generals.

Grant's most important supporter was President Abraham Lincoln. Lincoln recognized Grant's military talents early on. When Grant suffered heavy losses on the first day of the Battle of Shiloh in April 1862, people called for him to be replaced. Lincoln refused to do this, and his faith was rewarded by Grant's subsequent military successes. Lincoln promoted Grant several times before he finally made him general-in-chief of the Armies of the United States in March 1864.

COLLEAGUES: (left to right) General Sherman, Grant, President Lincoln, and Admiral David Porter discuss the war.

TRUSTED: William T. Sherman was Grant's most trusted general.

Grant's Officers

William T. Sherman served under Grant in 1862 and 1863 and became his most trusted general. The two men oversaw the capture of Vicksburg. When Grant became overall commander, Sherman became Union commander in the West. Grant sent Sherman to carry out a destructive march through the South. In contrast to Sherman, General George G. Meade, another of Grant's subordinates, was heavily criticized for his lack of aggression. His victory at Gettysburg was criticized because he allowed Lee's weakened forces to escape.

> " Grant is the greatest soldier of our time if not all time. "

William T. Sherman, 1885

A Lost Ally

Secretary of War Edwin M. Stanton campaigned for Grant to be president and Grant rewarded him with an appointment to the US Supreme Court in December 1869. Stanton died before he could be sworn in and robbed Grant of an important ally during his presidency.

LEE'S GENERALS

Robert E. Lee was an outstanding soldier who also commanded some of the leading generals of his generation.

Lee served as President Jefferson Davis's military advisor from the start of the war. In June 1862, he took command of the major Confederate army and renamed it the Army of Northern Virginia. Although Lee offered to resign after his defeat at the Battle of Gettysburg in July 1863, Davis refused to accept it.

Lee's army became the most successful of all Confederate armies, thanks to a group of remarkable commanders: Thomas "Stonewall" Jackson, James Longstreet, and J.E.B. "Jeb" Stuart.

Talented Officers

"Stonewall" Jackson proved himself an outstanding general with victories at Fredericksburg (December 1862) and Chancellorsville (May 1863). When Jackson died from pneumonia after being accidently shot after Chancellorsville, Lee was devastated.

PRESIDENT: Jefferson Davis relied on Lee in all military matters.

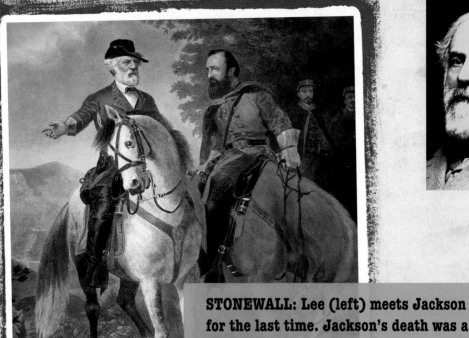

STONEWALL: Lee (left) meets Jackson for the last time. Jackson's death was a tragedy for Lee and for the South.

J.E.B. "Jeb" Stuart was a skilled cavalryman whose reconnaissance patrols were vital to Lee's success. The defeat at Gettysburg was caused in part because Stuart's scouting failed to detect the Union forces. When Stuart was fatally wounded defending Richmond in May 1864, Lee lost a key source of information.

Known as "My Old War Horse" by Lee, Longstreet took part in many battles throughout the war. But he later severely criticized Lee's tactics at Gettysburg. After Lee's surrender on April 12, 1865, the two former friends never spoke to each other again.

> " Lee is the greatest military genius in America, myself not excepted. "
>
> Union General Winfield Scott, 1870

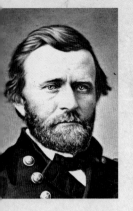

LINES ARE DRAWN

Lincoln did not recognize the right of the South to leave the Union. The creation of the Confederacy made civil war almost inevitable.

The first shots came at Fort Sumter, a federal fort in Charleston Harbor, South Carolina. After 34 hours of Confederate bombardment, the fort surrendered on April 19, 1861. Lincoln immediately called for 75,000 volunteers to join the Union Army. In the Battle of Bull Run on July 21, 1861, this army suffered a defeat that shocked the North. It was clear that the war would not be a short one.

Battle of Shiloh

On April 6, 1862, 40,000 Confederates surprised Grant at Shiloh, or Pittsburg Landing, on the Tennessee River. Grant's soldiers stood firm

SUMTER: Confederate guns blast Fort Sumter in April 1861.

ADVANCE: Union troops advance at Shiloh, Tennessee, in April 1862.

until Union reinforcements arrived on the second day. The battle was a turning point for Grant, whose victory relied on massive manpower and aggressive tactics, even when he was in danger of defeat.

Seven Days' Battles

By June 1862, Union soldiers under General McClellan were within striking distance of the Confederate capital, Richmond. But Robert E. Lee took control of the Confederate forces. He attacked McClellan and drove him away from Richmond.

" I appeal to all loyal citizens to favor, facilitate and aid this effort to maintain the honor, the integrity, and the existence of our National Union, and the perpetuity of popular government. "

Abraham Lincoln summons the militia, April 1861

MARYLAND CAMPAIGN

With a string of victories behind him, Lee invaded the North on September 4, 1862. It turned out to be a turning point in the war.

Lee hoped to achieve an easy victory over the North in Maryland. He hoped that would encourage Great Britain and France to recognize the Confederacy as an independent nation.

Battle of Antietam

The invasion started well, but Union General McClellan got hold of Lee's battle plans. McClellan's Army of the Potomac was waiting to meet Confederate troops at the Battle of South Mountain. However, McClellan did not launch a full-scale attack, which allowed Lee to reinforce his troops. Three days later, the two sides met at Antietam.

CLASH: At South Mountain, Union troops missed the chance to win a decisive victory.

ANTIETAM: Union troops capture a key bridge at Antietam.

A Bloody Battle

The Battle of Antietam (Sharpsburg) was fought on September 17, 1862. It remains the bloodiest single day in US history, with 23,000 soldiers killed, wounded, or missing in the heavy fighting. McClellan emerged as the victor, while Lee retreated back into Virginia.

A New War Aim

After the Confederate defeats at South Mountain and Antietam, Lincoln issued his preliminary Emancipation Proclamation. This promised that slaves in the South would be freed on January 1, 1863. The North was now fighting not just to preserve the Union, but also to abolish slavery.

> **"** I have heard of 'the dead lying in heaps,' but never saw it till this battle. Whole ranks fell together. **"**
>
> **Captain Emory Upton, 2nd US Artillery, at Antietam**

VICKSBURG

Vicksburg, Mississippi, sits on a bluff overlooking the Mississippi River. The city's strategic location made it vital to both sides.

The capture of Vicksburg would give the Union control of the Mississippi and split the Confederacy in two. Grant's campaign to capture the city was one of the most brilliant of the whole war. It led to his appointment as general-in-chief of the Union armies.

The Siege of Vicksburg

As Grant's Union forces converged on Vicksburg, they forced the Confederates, commanded by General John Pemberton, to retreat to the city after a series of defeats. Pemberton planned to remain in

ASSAULT: Union troops make an unsuccessful attack on Vicksburg in May.

FLEET: Admiral David Porter sails his gunboats past the batteries at Vicksburg.

Vicksburg until reinforcements arrived. Meanwhile, Grant maneuvered into position. He sent a fleet of gunboats past the Confederate batteries at night so that he could use them to ferry his men across the Mississippi south of the city.

> " Grant is my man, and I am his the rest of the war. "
>
> **Lincoln on Grant, July 5, 1863**

Under Siege

On May 19, 1863, Grant attacked Vicksburg but suffered heavy losses. Instead, he began a siege, ordering his soldiers to dig trenches around the city. For 47 days, Union artillery bombarded the city. In Vicksburg, soldiers and civilians suffered terribly. Eventually, with no more food and no hope of reinforcement, the Confederates surrendered Vicksburg on July 4. The Union now controlled the Mississippi River.

CHATTANOOGA

Chattanooga in Tennessee was known as the "Gateway to the South." Both sides fought hard to take control of it in summer and fall 1863.

The Confederates had halted the Union advance through Tennessee at the Battle of Chickamauga (September 19-20, 1863). They forced William S. Rosecrans' Army of the Cumberland back to Chattanooga.

The Siege of Chattanooga

Confederate General Braxton Bragg and his Army of Tennessee laid siege to Chattanooga. The Union forces ran low on supplies until October, when Ulysses S. Grant arrived. Newly promoted to be the Union commander in the West, Grant reinforced the troops and established a new supply line, called the "Cracker Line," into the city.

MOUNTAIN: Union troops attack Confederate positions on Lookout Mountain.

OBSERVATION: Grant and his generals watch their troops advance on Missionary Ridge.

Grant Takes the Offensive

With the help of General Sherman and four divisions who arrived in mid-November, Grant started his offensive. Union troops captured Orchard Knob and Lookout Mountain, driving out the Confederate forces. On November 25, 1863, the Union forces converged on the vital Missionary Ridge and defeated the remaining Confederates. With no safe positions left, Bragg ordered his men to retreat.

Important Base

In just 6 months, Union forces had succeeded in taking control of the "Gateway to the South" and had changed the course of the war. The Union troops now had the supply base they needed to launch an attack on Atlanta, Georgia, deep in Confederate territory.

> " I never saw troops move into action in finer style than Thomas's did today. "
>
> **John Rawlins, Grant's chief of staff, Missionary Ridge, 1863**

GETTYSBURG

The largest and bloodiest battle of the Civil War, Gettysburg was to end Robert E. Lee's second invasion of the North.

The Battle of Gettysburg started by chance when the opposing forces met each other at Gettysburg, Pennsylvania. After 3 days of fighting, from July 1–3, 1863, it was clear that the Confederacy no longer had any chance of winning the war. The high cost of life led to President Abraham Lincoln visiting Gettysburg in November 1863 to take part in the dedication of a new cemetery for fallen Union soldiers. He gave a brief speech that has become one of the most famous speeches in US history: the Gettysburg Address.

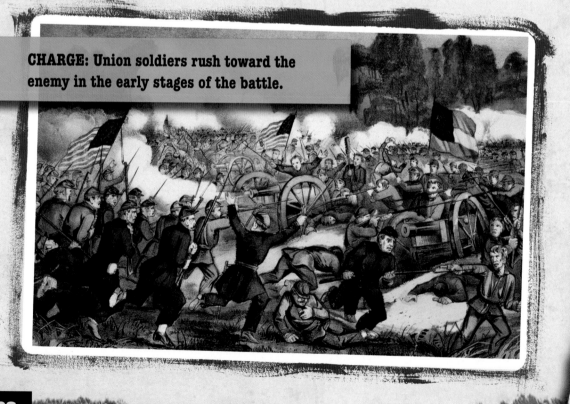

CHARGE: Union soldiers rush toward the enemy in the early stages of the battle.

BATTLEFIELD: Little Round Top was a key part of the high ground near the town.

A Second Invasion

On June 16, 1863, Lee ordered the Army of Northern Virginia to cross the Potomac River to start a second invasion of the North. He planned to march through Maryland into Pennsylvania, and then on to Washington, DC. His army numbered around 75,000 soldiers, including three infantry corps and J.E.B. Stuart's cavalry corps.

> **"** We entered Gettysburg in the afternoon, just in time to meet the enemy entering the town, and in good season to drive him back before his getting a foothold. **"**

John Buford, Union cavalry officer

A Chance Encounter

Gettysburg lay on an important junction of roads that led to Washington, DC, Baltimore, and Harrisburg, the capital of Pennsylvania. Early on July 1, Confederates foraging close to the town clashed with a Union cavalry brigade. It soon became clear that both sides had major armies in the area.

> **" It's all my fault. It is I who have lost this fight. "**
>
> **Robert E. Lee, July 3, 1863**

The First Two Days

Once Robert E. Lee and his opposing leader, General George G. Meade, learned their armies had met, they both sent for reinforcements. On the first day, Lee's men succeeded in driving Union troops through Gettysburg and onto the high ground at Cemetery Ridge, south of the town. By July 2, Meade had more than 90,000 men consolidating their positions on the higher ground. Despite suffering severe losses in fierce fighting around Devil's Den and the Peach Orchard, the Union line managed to hold. The Confederates gained ground, but on July 3, the Union soldiers regained the ground they had lost the previous day in continued fighting at Culp's Hill.

DEFENSE: Union defenders hold their line in the face of Pickett's Charge.

DEFEAT: Gettysburg was the last major campaign in which the Confederates were on the offensive.

Pickett's Charge

On the afternoon of July 3, Lee made a fateful decision. He ordered General James Longstreet to break the Union line at Cemetery Ridge. In what became known as Pickett's Charge—named for Longstreet's subordinate, General George Pickett—some 15,000 men attacked across a mile (1.6 km) of open ground toward Union troops protected by a stone wall. Union artillery fired on the slow-moving advance. Only a few Confederates survived to reach the wall, where they faced withering rifle fire.

Retreat to Virginia

Lee had made a huge tactical error. The next day, he ordered his men to retreat to Virginia. More than 20,000 Confederate soldiers were killed, wounded, or missing. Union casualties stood at 23,000. The Confederates would be on the defensive for the rest of the war.

OVERLAND CAMPAIGN

Over 6 weeks in summer 1864, Grant and Lee became direct opponents for the first time, as they tried to outmaneuver one another.

Grant was now the general-in-chief of all the Union armies. He planned an overland advance on Richmond that would either capture the Confederate capital or destroy Lee's army.

On May 5-7, 1864, the two sides met in the dense forest known as the Wilderness at Spotsylvania. The battle was a bloody stalemate. At Cold Harbor in early June, the Confederates were victorious.

WILDERNESS: Thick forest and scrub made fighting hard at Spotsylvania.

REST: Union troops enjoy a moment to relax during the assault on Petersburg.

Having failed to destroy the Army of Northern Virginia or to take Richmond, Grant switched his attention to Petersburg. If he captured this important transportation hub, Lee would be forced either to evacuate Richmond or to fight Grant with far fewer soldiers. Between June 15-18, 1864, however, 42,000 Confederates beat back 62,000 Union troops from Petersburg.

Outstanding General

Throughout the Overland Campaign, Lee had proved that he was tactically the equal of Grant—if not his superior. But Grant had more men and enough resources to simply keep fighting. Despite the failure of his campaign, he never entertained the possibility that his Union forces might lose the war.

> **I may be mistaken but I feel that our success over Lee's army is already assured.**

Ulysses S. Grant, 1864

THE SURRENDER

The first days of April 1865 saw the final campaign of the Civil War and the defeat of Lee's Army of Northern Virginia.

By the spring of 1865, Grant's Union armies were in control. Under Grant's orders, General William T. Sherman had marched his army through Georgia and the Carolinas, destroying everything in his path. This "March to the Sea" met little opposition, but it left the Confederate armies even shorter of men and supplies.

ISOLATED: Defeat in the Battle of Five Forks left Lee in danger of being cut off.

TRUCE: This contemporary drawing shows Confederates approaching Union officers to discuss a truce.

Lee's Last Stand

Lee was determined to fight on. On April 2, 1865, however, at the Battle of Five Forks, Grant cut off the final supply line to Petersburg. Lee was forced to evacuate Petersburg and to abandon the Confederate capital at Richmond, which fell to Union troops.

Lee planned to head west and regroup at Amelia Court House, where supplies would be waiting. From there, he intended to head south in order to meet up with General Joseph E. Johnston's Army of Tennessee, which had been facing Sherman in North Carolina.

Grant's Plan

Grant anticipated Lee's plan. He sent General Philip H. Sheridan to cut off Lee's direct route. Sensing that victory was near, Grant decided that

> ❝ **Hold Five Forks at all hazards. I regret exceedingly your forces' withdrawal.** ❞
>
> **Robert E. Lee to General Pickett, April 2, 1865**

he would attempt to cut off Lee's troops, surround them, and force a surrender. This would avoid another large battle, and the loss of more men on both sides.

Hungry Men

Lee arrived at Amelia Court House on April 4, but the supplies had not arrived. He ordered his men south, but Sheridan forced them west across the Appomattox River. By now, Lee's men were very hungry. Exhausted soldiers collapsed as they marched. Confederate supplies had reached Appomattox, but Sheridan seized them. Lee was surrounded. Although some of his junior officers wanted to fight on, Lee refused to sacrifice more men. He had no choice but to go to see Grant and discuss the terms of a surrender.

FOES: Lee (left) signs the surrender, watched by Grant (seated, right).

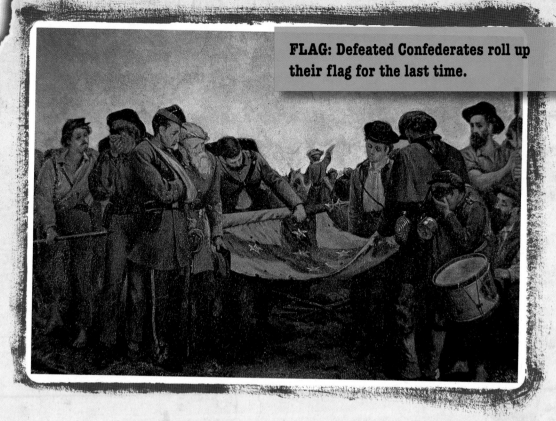

FLAG: Defeated Confederates roll up their flag for the last time.

FLAG: Defeated Confederates roll up their flag for the last time.

Surrender Ceremony

At 1:00 P.M. on April 9, Lee rode to Appomattox Court House to meet Grant. The surrender took 3 days. Lee agreed to Grant's terms, which allowed Union officers to keep their horses and personal weapons. Grant ordered that the Union men present should not celebrate the surrender. On April 12, 1865, the Army of Northern Virginia marched out for the last time to lay down its arms and battle flags in a formal ceremony. Union bugles saluted the defeated Confederates. Within 3 months all Confederate forces would stop fighting. The Civil War was over.

> **"The Confederates were now our prisoners, and we did not want to exult over their downfall."**
>
> Ulysses S. Grant, 1865

PRESIDENT GRANT

Ulysses S. Grant was hailed as a hero and savior of the United States. He continued to serve his country for the rest of his life.

President Andrew Johnson named Grant as his Secretary of War in the newly united country. In 1868, Grant ran against Johnson in the presidential election and won, becoming the 18th President of the United States. Grant served two terms. His time in office was overshadowed by corruption and scandal, although he was not personally involved. Although he had been an outstanding soldier, Grant often seemed to be out of his depth as president.

POSTER: This poster shows Grant with his running mate, John Schuyler Colfax.

GRANT: At work on his memoirs less than a month before his death in July 1885.

Life After the White House

After leaving office, Grant made a 2-year world tour. He was greeted as a hero wherever he went. Back in the United States, he became a partner in a financial firm. When it went bust, he was left bankrupt. About the same time, he learned he had throat cancer. Grant decided to write his memoirs to pay off his debts and leave some money for his family. Soon after completing a two-volume memoir, Grant died, aged 63, on July 23, 1885, in Wilton, New York.

Thirty days of national mourning followed. Grant's body was placed on a special train and taken to New York City, via West Point. A quarter of a million people filed past his coffin. Despite his problems as president, Grant remained a national hero.

> **This war was a fearful lesson, and should teach us the necessity of avoiding wars in the future.**
>
> **Ulysses S. Grant, 1885**

ACADEMIC CAREER

Pardoned by Lincoln after he surrendered on April 9, Lee worked hard to ensure that civil war would never be repeated.

When the war ended, Lee and his family could not return to the family estate at Arlington, Virginia. It was now in the middle of a US National Cemetery for fallen soldiers.

Washington College

Instead, the family moved to Lexington, Virginia, where Lee had accepted an offer to become president of a small educational institution, Washington College. For the rest of his life Lee worked hard to improve the college and the lives of his students.

REUNION: Lee (front, second left) meets some of his generals after the war.

TOMB: Robert E. Lee was buried with full military honors.

Lee tried to ensure that his fellow Southerners accepted that they were again citizens of the United States. He urged them not to be bitter but to rebuild the country. For his part, he signed an amnesty oath in 1865, asking to become a US citizen again.

> " Dismiss from your mind all sectional feeling, and bring your children up to be Americans. "
>
> Robert E. Lee to a Confederate widow, circa 1866

Poor Health

The effects of the war and the hard work Lee put into Washington College started to take their toll. A heart condition that had affected him since the end of the war grew worse. In September 1870, he suffered a massive stroke. Two weeks later, on October 12, Lee died at Washington College. His funeral took place in Lexington. His beloved Traveller, the horse he had ridden since 1862, followed his casket.

AFTERMATH

As the difficult job of reuniting the country got underway, the assassination of President Abraham Lincoln threw things into disarray.

The process of reuniting the country, called Reconstruction, fell first to President Andrew Johnson then to President Ulysses S. Grant. Although Robert E. Lee played no public role, in private he advised his fellow former Confederates to put past differences aside in order to preserve the Union.

As Johnson began Reconstruction, Grant still commanded the US Army. He carried out Congressional plans to reoccupy the South and held elections there in 1867 in which former African American slaves

CARPETBAGGER: Southerners resented Northerners who headed South to seize political power.

TERROR: The Ku Klux Klan sets fire to a school for African Americans.

were allowed to vote. Johnson had gone back on Abraham Lincoln's promise to build a nation "with malice toward none, with charity for all" by trying to limit African-American rights, but Congress passed the Fourteenth Amendment against the president's wishes, making African Americans US citizens.

Grant's Presidency

As president, Grant acted more in the spirit of Lincoln than of Johnson. He led Reconstruction by signing and enforcing civil rights legislation. Grant also fought against the rise of the Ku Klux Klan, which was an anti-African American organization in the South whose members included former Confederate soldiers. The Ku Klux Klan used terror tactics such as lynching to try to stop African Americans from voting. Grant continued to insist that African Americans had the same rights as white Americans and were equally entitled to vote.

> **I would protect the law-abiding citizen, whether of native or foreign birth.**
>
> **President Grant, 1869, First Inaugural Address**

JUDGMENT

GRANT Vs. LEE

Who fought a better war? General Grant led the Union to victory but General Lee proved time and again he was a brilliant military strategist.

* Grant's military strategy was helped by the Union's superiority in industry, transportation, and manpower.

* Lincoln admired Grant's single-minded aggressiveness toward the enemy.

* Grant believed the war could only be won by showing the South how brutal war really was. That was why he sent Sherman to march through the South, destroying whatever he found.

TERRITORY

TERRITORY

KS

RI COM
INDIA
TERRIT

Although the Confederates were defeated in the war, Robert E. Lee won many notable victories with forces that were usually smaller and less well equipped than those of his opponents.

* Lee is generally considered the most brilliant soldier of his generation.

* Lee knew the Confederates would have to invade the North if they were to win the war.

* Lee's first invasion was stopped at Antietam after the Union got hold of Lee's orders. The second ended with Lee's misjudgment at Gettysburg.

* Lee accepted in April 1865 that it was the right time to surrender in order to avoid further casualties.

TIMELINE

Both Grant and Lee played key roles throughout much of the Civil War. They only came into direct conflict toward the end of the conflict, after Grant was promoted in March 1864.

Taking Sides
In April, after Virginia secedes, Robert E. Lee resigns from the US Army and takes command of Confederate forces in Virginia.

Saving Richmond
In May, Robert E. Lee takes command of the Army of Northern Virginia after General Joseph E. Johnston is wounded. From June to August, Lee drives back Union forces from Richmond, Virginia.

A Costly Defeat
In September, Lee invades the North for the first time but suffers a strategic defeat at the Battle of Antietam.

1861

1862

1863

Slow Rise
In June, Ulysses S. Grant becomes a commander of volunteers in Illinois; he is later promoted.

Promotion for Grant
After Grant's victories at Fort Donelson in February and Shiloh in April, in October he becomes commander of Tennessee and begins a campaign to capture Vicksburg.

Tragic Loss
Lee wins a series of victories including, in May, the Battle of Chancellorsville. The victory, however, costs the life of Southern hero Thomas "Stonewall" Jackson.

Lee's Misjudgment
In July, Lee invades the North again. He makes an error of judgment at the Battle of Gettysburg that costs him any possible victory. Davis refuses Lee's letter of resignation.

Grant Takes Charge
In March, Grant is made commander of all the Union forces. He begins to plan a campaign of attrition based on the North's advantage in manpower and supplies.

End of Resistance
In April, Lee loses control of Petersburg and Richmond. His attempts to escape finally lead to Appomattox Court House, Virginia.

1864　　　　　**1865**

Fall of Vicksburg
In July, Vicksburg surrenders after a brilliant campaign by Grant and a long siege. In October, Grant takes command of all Union forces in the West.

Target Richmond
In the Overland Campaign, a series of 12 battles in just 7 weeks, Lee shows he can outmaneuver Grant, but Grant's better resources give him the advantage.

Surrender
On April 9, Lee surrenders to Grant at Appomattox Court House, Virginia.

GLOSSARY

abolitionist Someone campaigning to have slavery made illegal.

artillery Heavy guns such as cannon and mortars.

battery A group of artillery weapons, often in a strongpoint, that are used together.

brigade A section of an army made up of infantry regiments.

bombardment A constant attack with artillery shells and missiles.

forage To search an area to try to find food or provisions.

gunboat A small, fast river vessel with guns mounted on it.

lynching The illegal killing of someone by a group of people, usually by hanging.

memoirs A historical account written from personal knowledge.

militia Volunteer soldiers who serve as civilians in the military.

plantation A large estate for growing crops such as tobacco or cotton.

reconnaissance Observing the enemy to gather information.

Reconstruction The period following the Civil War, from 1865 to 1877.

reinforcements Extra soldiers sent to increase the strength of a unit or army.

secession The act of withdrawing from membership of an organization.

sectional Relating to part of something rather than the whole.

siege A military operation in which armed forces surround a position or city in order to force it to surrender.

stalemate A contest in which neither side is able to win a victory.

strategy A plan to achieve a long-term goal rather than an immediate result.

tactic An action or plan made for immediate rather than long-term purposes.

FOR FURTHER INFORMATION

Books

Ford, Carin T. *An Overview of the American Civil War Through Primary Sources*. (The Civil War Through Primary Sources). Enslow Publishers, 2013.

George, Enzo. *The Civil War: War Between Brothers* (Voices of War). Cavendish Square Publishing, 2014.

Kent, Zachary. *The Civil War: From Fort Sumter to Appomattox* (The United States at War). Enslow Publishing, Inc, 2011.

McNeese, Tim. *Civil War Battles* (The Civil War: A Nation Divided). Chelsea House Publishers, 2009.

Ratliffe, Thomas. *You Wouldn't Want to be a Civil War Soldier*. Turtleback, 2013.

Samuels, Charlie. *Timeline of the Civil War* (Americans at War). Gareth Stevens Publishing, 2011.

Websites

http://www.pbs.org/civilwar/
Extensive website to support the PBS documentary film *The Civil War*, by Ken Burns.

http://www.history.com/topics/american-civil-war/robert-e-lee
History.com page with a biography and videos about Robert E. Lee.

http://www.history.com/topics/us-presidents/ulysses-s-grant
History.com page with a biography and videos about Ulysses S. Grant, both in the Civil War and as president of the United States.

http://www.historyplace.com/civilwar/index.html
Civil War timelines on The History Place website.

Publisher's note to educators and parents: Our editors have carefully reviewed these websites to ensure that they are suitable for students. Many websites change frequently, however, and we cannot guarantee that a site's future contents will continue to meet our high standards of quality and educational value. Be advised that students should be closely supervised whenever they access the Internet.

INDEX